The Amazing Book

For Girls Online

make

bake &

create

The Amazing Book For Girls Online: make, bake & create
A girl's essential DIY lifestyle book. Ideas for creating everything from blueberry bath bombs to emoji cookies, chocolate facemasks & fairy light lanterns.

Created By Christina Rose
Creative Direction: Daisy Bell

Contributors: shutterstock/R_lion_O, shutterstock/alicedaniel, shutterstock/lineartestpilot, shutterstock/ blue67design, shutterstock/topform, shutterstock/ Christos Georghiou, shutterstock/Marie Nimrichterova, shutterstock/ Ohn Mar, shutterstock/mirrelley, shutterstock/Alexcardo, shutterstock/ mirrelley, shutterstock/Yuliya Verovski, shutterstock/Mariart32, shutterstock/ Khabarushka, shutterstock/davorana, shutterstock/Creative Stall, shutterstock/ lukepedclub, shutterstock/ chotwit piyapramote, shutterstock/ Kollibri, shutterstock/ Anna Kutukova, shutterstock/Negritosik, shutterstock/ solgas, shutterstock/wildfloweret, shutterstock/Missgraphic, shutterstock/ Tidarat Tiemjai, shutterstock/Darii-s, shutterstock/Drakonyashka, shutterstock/ Tanyastock, shutterstock/pandora64, shutterstock/GooseFrol, shutterstock/ Yellow Stocking, shutterstock/paween, shutterstock/ Tatyana Kyul, shutterstock/Lauritta, shutterstock/NoraVector, shutterstock/Talirina, shutterstock/Les Perysty, shutterstock/Zhe Vasylieva, shutterstock/Sapunkele, shutterstock/tapilipa, shutterstock/chotwit piyapramote, shutterstock/ Anna Isaeva, shutterstock/TheYellowBee, shutterstock/ Vekilan, shutterstock/ zsooofija, shutterstock/ vectorfairy, shutterstock/ Ksusha Dusmikeeva, shutterstock/ Timashov Sergiy, shutterstock/AlexLMX, shutterstock/ LAR01JoKa, shutterstock/Andriy Lipkan, shutterstock/Chones, shutterstock/MatoomMi, shutterstock/art designer, shutterstock/ wenchiawang, shutterstock/Politchka, shutterstock/Suchkova Anna, shutterstock/ Mushroompicker's shop, shutterstock/punsayaporn, shutterstock/ Natasha_Chetkova, shutterstock/E.K, shutterstock/ ykononova, shutterstock/ Anna.zabella, shutterstock/ Kalenik Hanna, shutterstock/ Alias Ching.

First published in the United Kingdom in 2015 by
Bell & Mackenzie Publishing Limited

ISBN: 978-1-910771-66-2

www.bellmackenzie.com

Contents

Honey & Chocolate Face Mask

you'll need...

2 teaspoons cocoa powder
2 teaspoons Greek yogurt
2 teaspoons runny honey

now make it....

In a bowl mix together all the ingredients. Make sure you combine it really well because cocoa powder can be tricky to blend smoothly. Keep on going until you have got what looks like melted chocolate and then you'll know it's ready

As with all face masks give your face a little rinse with warm water and dab it dry. Then you are ready to apply the chocolate carefully all over your face, use your finger or a wooden paddle. Be careful to keep it away from your eyes.

Now it's time to chill and relax for half an hour while you let your mask do its thing!

After this time wash it off with lukewarm water and dab your face dry. All finished...... bet your skin feels good now?!

perfect with a
glass of milk!

emoji cookies

you'll need...

- cookie mix
- Mixing Bowl
- Flour
- Hand mixer
- Rolling pin
- circular cookie cutter
- Baking tray
- yellow, black, white, pink icing tubes

now make it....

Use a cookie mix for this - it's easier, quicker and makes everything more fun! chose whichever type you like best, usually you'll only need to add water but check the back of the packet because you might need an egg too!

First thing to do is heat the oven up. Set it to about 170C/370F/ Gas3 or whatever your packet says.

Get the cookie mix and water all stirred up together in a big bowl until you have nice dough (which isn't too sticky).

sprinkle a bit of flour on the work top and roll out the dough. Use the cutter to cut them into your Emoji circles and place on them a baking tray.

Bake for about 5-7 minutes until the edges are golden brown (check that's what you're your packet says if not follow the instructions to make sure you get your cookies perfect).

If they have spread a bit when they come out of the oven use your cutter again to make then a circle shape.

Let them cool off for about half an hour on a cooling rack.

Grab your yellow icing and make an outline right around the edge of the cookie. Leave it for a minute or two to harden and then fill in the rest of the cookie with lots more yellow icing, long lines up and down are best to give you a completely yellow Emoji.

Now it's the fun part use black, white & pink icing to express your favourite Emoji faces and give your cookies attitude!

Avocado & Honey Hair Repair

This is deep conditioning DIY style. It takes an hour or two to complete and if you make it part of your weekly hair routine you'll adore the difference it makes plus it stimulates hair growth and we all LOVE that!

2 teaspoons runny honey
2 teaspoons extra virgin olive oil
half a ripe avocado
shower cap

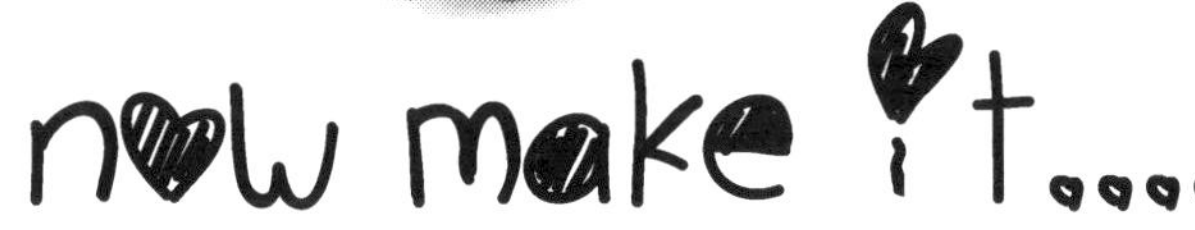

scoop the avocado flesh out into a bowl. Make sure it's good and ripe (if you've got really long hair use a whole avocado).

use a fork to mash it to a creamy paste. Really mash it well as if you were going to eat it as a smooth dip. No chunks allowed! Add the honey and olive oil and mix it up until everything is combined.

scoop some into your hand and start working it into the ends. when you've worked it through grab some more and start applying to the top of your head and all the way down the back and sides of your hair. work it right through everywhere, make sure you get underneath too, but give the greatest attention to the ends as they the are most damaged part of your hair.

when you have really worked it in good, tie your hair up into a messy bun, put a shower cap over the top and leave for about an hour.

After the hour is up (you can even leave it for 2 hours if you like) jump in the shower and give you hair a good wash as usual with shampoo and conditioner. welcome to healthy hair!

Pancake Stack

now make it....

Use the whisk to beat the eggs and sugar together in a bowl. Add the melted butter and keep beating for a minute or two. Add the vanilla extract & milk and carry on beating.

Sift the flour into the bowl. Add the salt and whisk together until everything is nice and smooth.

Add a couple of drops of olive oil to the frying pan, spread it around with a piece of kitchen roll and place the pan on a medium heat, you don't want it to be too hot.

Let the pan heat up and then use the ladle to scoop out some of the pancake batter. Pour it into the pan, cook for a minute or two and then flip over with the spatula. Cook for another minute or two until both sides are golden brown.

Put your cooked pancake on the plate and get some more going to make your stack (keep the plate and pancakes warm in the oven if you like while you are making the rest).

you'll need...

6oz flour
2 eggs
2oz melted butter (you can gently melt the butter on a low heat in a pan while you are getting everything else together)
1 cup milk
2oz sugar
1 teaspoon vanilla extract
half teaspoon salt
3 teaspoons baking powder
Olive Oil
Mixing bowl
Whisk
Frying pan
Spatula
Ladle or big serving spoon
Sieve

The mix should make about 8-10 pancakes so you'll have to guess how much to use for each pancake. I'd say the ladle should have about 2 tablespoons of mixture in it but it's really up to you how big you want your pancakes to be.

Eat with maple syrup, jam, honey, whipped cream or whatever you like best. Yummy!

1 Minute Microwave Mug-Muffins

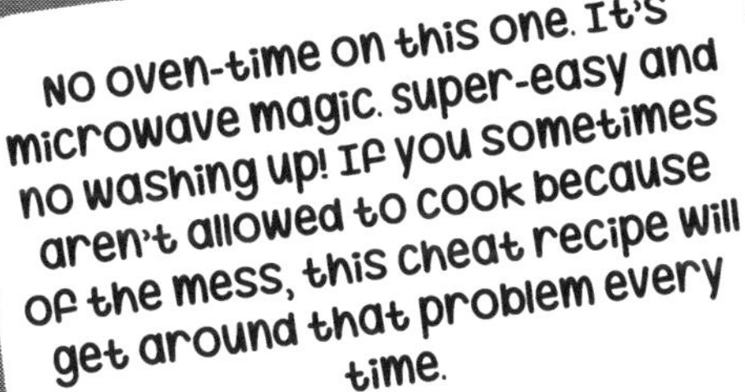

No oven-time on this one. It's microwave magic. super-easy and no washing up! If you sometimes aren't allowed to cook because of the mess, this cheat recipe will get around that problem every time.

This quantity will make enough for 2 cakes so get 2 mugs ready. You'll use one for mixing and then split the mixture between them.

you'll need...

2 tablespoons butter
1 egg
2 tablespoons milk
1 teaspoon pure vanilla extract
2oz granulated sugar
2oz self-raising flour
(Add a teaspoon of cocoa powder for chocolate sponge)

now make it....

Place the butter in a mug and heat for 20 seconds in the microwave or until it's melted. crack the egg into the mug, Stir it well with a fork to make sure you break up the yolk and combine it well with the melted butter.

Add all the other ingredients and mix well with a fork. Divide the cake mix between the two mugs and microwave each one separately for about 50 seconds each or until the batter rises up and looks like a cake.

The choice now is to eat it right there hot with a fork or let it cool off and decorate with frosting and tons of sprinkles. or how about this?? Eat one right now and let the other one cool off before decorating. Get the best of both worlds!

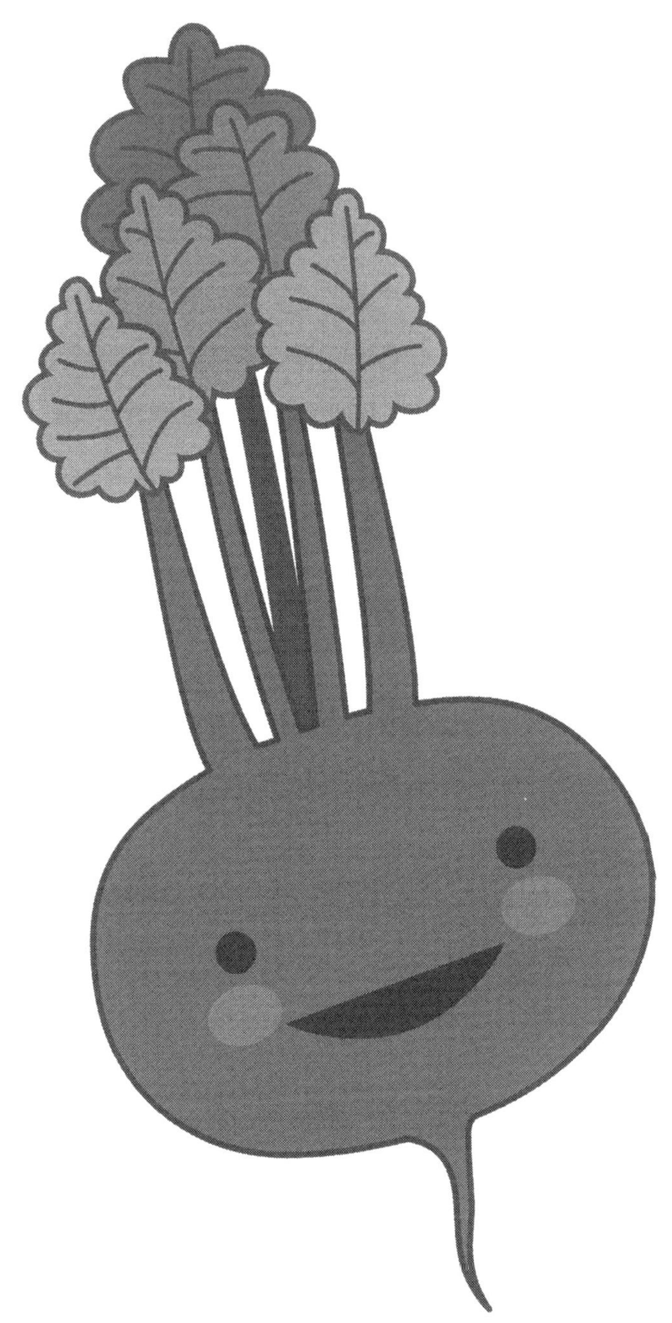

Natural Beetroot Lip Tint

you'll need...

1 fresh beetroot bulb
sharp knife

Slice the end of your beetroot to expose the pretty red flesh underneath. Cut a really thin slice off the bulb and then holding it in your hands dab/wipe the beetroot directly on to your lips. Be careful here not to get any on your face, you only want it on your lips. That's all you need to do. Ruby red and super simple. Keep the rest of the beetroot in the fridge and do the same everyday. Easy!

Tip: If you find it tricky applying the slice of beetroot straight onto your lips try using a cotton bud to apply the juice instead, you might find that a bit easier to start with. Just dab the bud onto the beetroot, let it absorb some juice and then apply it on to your lips using the bud as you would with any lipstick or lip balm.

DRINK
A
SMOOTHIE
EVERYDAY

Berry & Banana Smoothie

you'll need...

7oz mixed berries
1 banana
2 teaspoon honey
half cup milk

Rinse all the ingredients well. Peel the banana and break into small pieces.
Add the fruit, milk and honey to the blender. Top up with water.
Twist on the blade and blend until smooth.

Tip: Try using almond or soy milk for a different taste.

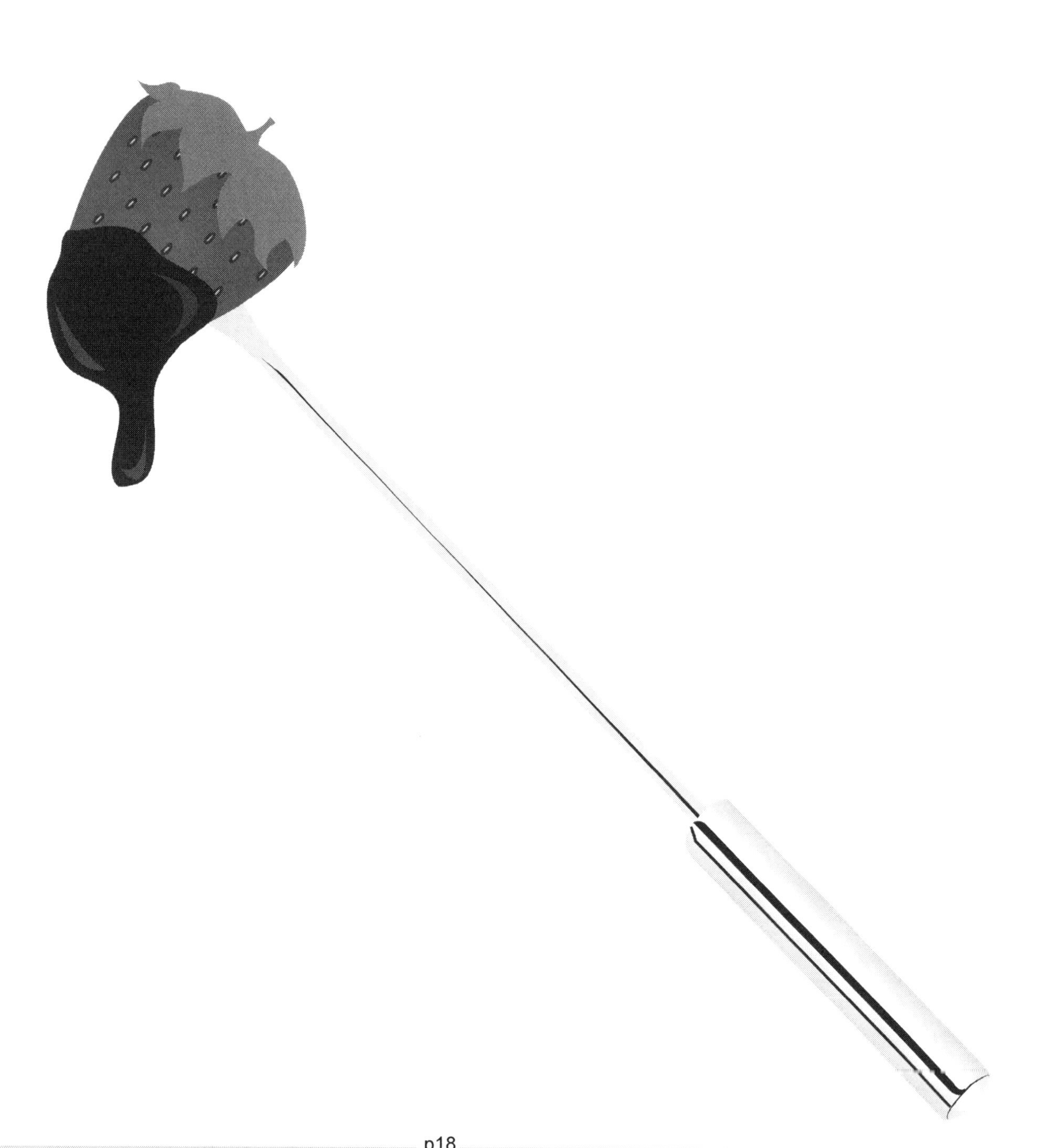

Chocolate Strawberry Fondue

you'll need...

three quarters cup of cream
7oz bar of chocolate broken up into pieces (use good quality chocolate)
1 tablespoon of unsalted butter
fresh strawberries or your favourite fruit
wooden skewers/sticks

now make it....

The first thing you need to do is take your strawberries out of the fridge. for a while so that they warm to room temperature. Remove the green tops and put the strawberries on a plate along with the wooden sticks.

Next place the cream in a saucepan and gently heat until it starts simmering. Add the chocolate and whisk or quickly stir until it's melted and smooth. Add the butter and whisk this too until everything is silky.

Next you need to pour the chocolate fondue into a bowl. Set it out on the table with your plate of strawberries.

Now it's time for everyone to grab a strawberry on a stick, dip and dig in!

Homemade Christmas Candle

you'll need...

candle wax flakes (or just melt down a plain candle)
1 tablespoon ground cinnamon
1 tablespoon vanilla extract
1 red crayon
1 candle wick
Glass jar

warning: Please be super-careful when making this candle. Always get permission from your parents, or responsible adult, before and never leave a naked flame unattended.

now make it....

Gently heat a nonstick saucepan on the cooker and add the wax flakes (or the plain candle). Break up the crayon and add this too. When everything starts melting add the cinnamon and vanilla. Carry on very gently heating until everything is melted and combined together and starts to smell lovely.

Meanwhile prepare your candle wick. Place the metal end of the wick so it rests inside the bottom of the jar. Wrap the top of the wick around a wood skewer or pencil and balance the skewer on the top of the jar to hold the wick in place while your candle sets. (Make sure the metal part is still resting on the base of the jar).

When the wax is melted and you have an even colour pour it into the jar being careful not to disturb the wick.

Leave to set overnight and then when it's ready unwind the wick from the pencil and trim it with some scissors so you should have just a little of the wick showing at the top of the candle

Tip: If you like you can wrap a ribbon around the jar to make it look especially pretty.

Donut Desk Coasters

These coasters are soooooo cute, super-easy to make and great to giveaway as gifts.

you'll need...

1 thin sheet of cork
Mod Podge glue
Paint Brushes
Colourful acrylic paint
scissors

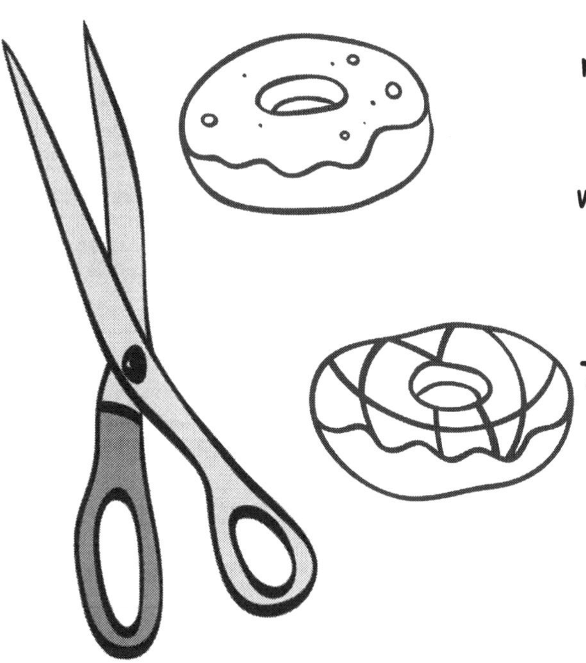

now make it....

Use a jam jar lid (or something else circular) to mark out the outline of donut shapes on the cork board. Use a smaller round shape (bottle lid or something) to make the whole in the centre of your ring donuts.

Use scissors to carefully cut out the outlines so you are left with cork donut shapes.

Draw the shape of some icing onto your donuts with a pen and then colour them in with the acrylic paints, make them as bright as you can, paint on sprinkles or whatever your fave toppings are to make them look really authentic.

When you are happy with the designs and they've dried off use a clean brush to paint glue over the top. This will seal it and give a waterproof glaze to your coaster.

Tip: Thin sheets of cork are available in craft/hobby shops or you can buy them cheaply online.

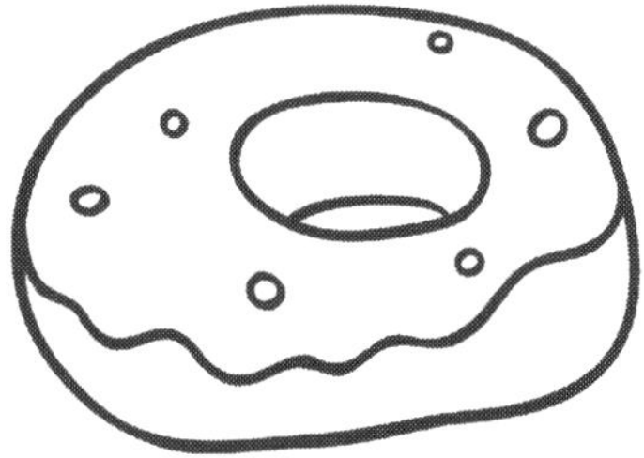

DIY Lipstick

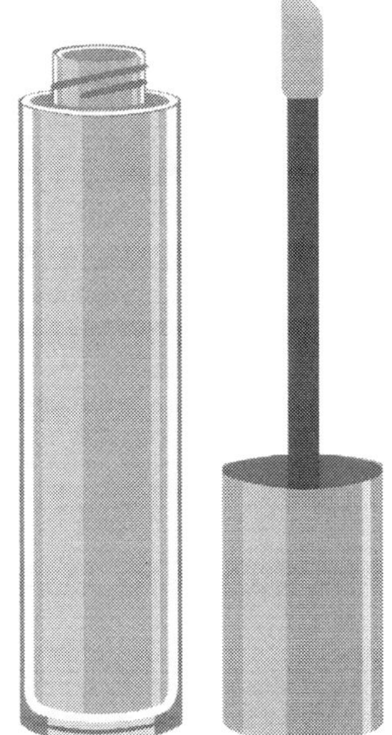

you'll need...

1 crayon (choose whichever colour you want to make your lipstick)
1 teaspoon of vaseline
small cute container

now make it....

Heat a pan and pour an inch or two of water into the base. Add a small bowl or dish which will sit in the base of the pan but won't get water in it.

While the water is gently heating peel the crayon wrapper and break it up into little pieces. Place this in the bowl which is sitting in the base of the pan and add the vaseline.

Over the next few minutes it will gently melt, stir it with a cocktail stick and when it's completely melted remove the dish and pour the liquid into your container.

That's it! Once it cools and sets it's homemade DIY lipstick.

So with a packet of crayons and a tub of vaseline you have got yourself an unlimited supply of lipstick in every colour of the rainbow and more!

Easy Bath Bomb

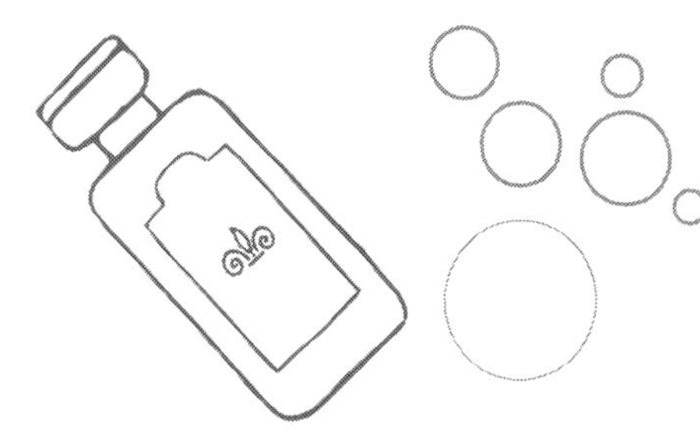

you'll need...

Dry Stuff:
6oz baking soda
3oz corn flour
3oz citric acid
3oz epsom salts
egg-shaped mould/container
(It sounds like there are some weird ingredients here but you can buy all this in the store)

Wet Stuff:
1 teaspoons essential oils (use lavender, peppermint or whatever you like best)
half teaspoon water
2 teaspoon coconut oil
A few drops food colouring (to make it look pretty)

now make it....

First mix all the dry ingredients together in a bowl. In a seperate bowl mix all the wet ingredients together.

Carefully drop the wet mix into the dry mix just a drop at a time and gently combine together with your hands (only do a little tiny bit at a time otherwise you'll have a chemical reaction before you want it).

When you've got what looks like sand, load it into your container. Make sure there is no space and it is tightly packed in. Leave for 24 hours to solidify. After this carefully remove from it's container and it's ready to use.

Ideally you'll be able to find a small bath bomb shaped container which splits into two, if not just use whatever shape you can find.

Tip: pack in a little box with some pretty tissue paper to give away as a gift

DIY Peppermint Lip scrub

This is a really easy fun thing to do. Be careful with the food colouring you choose though, you don't want to end up with blue lips!!!

you'll need...

1 drop peppermint food flavouring
1-2 drops food colouring (if you want the scrub to have a colour, chose whichever you like best)
1 tablespoon sugar
half teaspoon olive oil
Mixing bowl
Tiny cute container

now make it....

Add the sugar & olive oil to the bowl and mix it up with a small spoon.

Add the peppermint food flavouring, mix it in then finally add a drop or two of whichever food colouring you have chosen. when everything is mixed up and the colour is even you are good to go! spoon it into the cutest, tiniest container you can find. Label it up and get scrubbing!

Keep in mind the food colouring may give your lips a temporary tint SO BE CAREFUL with your colour choice or leave it out all together and you'll just have clear minty lip scrub!

happiness is homemade

Fairy Light Firefly Mason Jar

This really is so easy to do. It's quick and simple but has a magical feel making it seem like you have got a jar of fireflies in your own bedroom.

you'll need...

1 mason jar with lid (a mason jar is great but any jar will do)
Mod Podge glue
Sticky tape
Paint brush
L.E.D. fairy lights

now make it....

Using the brush paint the inside of the jar with glue, make sure you cover every inch then let it dry off.

Stick the battery part of the led lights to the inside of the lid using the sticky tape. Place the lights inside the jar, turn them on and close over the lid.

That's it, all done. Sit and enjoy the lovely warm glassy light from your fairy-light fireflies.

Tip: Use a small string of battery powered L.E.D. lights. You can pick them up super cheap.

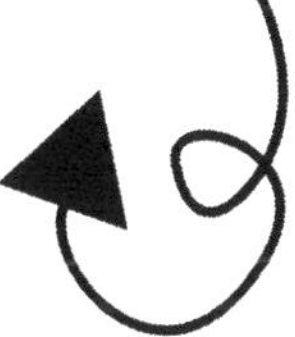

Edible Chocolate Bowl Set

you'll need...

4 balloons
1 x 7oz bar of milk chocolate broken up into pieces (use good quality chocolate)

Gently melt the chocolate. As mentioned elsewhere the best way to do this is to place it in a glass bowl which is sitting over a pan of simmering water ..it's quite boring though waiting for all the chocolate to slowly melt so you could just cheat by putting it in a bowl and whacking it in the microwave. Heat it for just a few seconds at a time though, checking each time to make sure it's melting but not burning.

While the chocolate is melting blow up your balloon. Once the chocolate is ready dip the smooth top of your balloon into the chocolate as deeply as you want your finished bowl to be.

Place the balloon on a plate and leave the chocolate to harden.

Repeat the steps above with the other three balloons.

When the chocolate on all the balloons has hardened, gently burst the balloons and carefully remove any trace of the balloons from your chocolate bowls. If you are careful what you should be left with a super cool edible bowl set which you can use to serve snacks to your friends and family.

Homemade Lemonade

you'll need...

½ lemon (or 2 tablespoons of lemon juice)
1 tablespoon sugar
1 cup water
Handful of ice cubes
Blender

now make it....

Rinse the lemon well, remove any pips and chop. Add everything to the blender, twist on the blade and blend until smooth.

Tip: Alter the amount of sugar to get the taste right. you could add some strawberries too for pink lemonade.

Homemade lemonade is a truly authentic drink. To make it look supercool serve it in a mason jar with a straw and some fresh mint.

Haribo Ice Pops

These are a really cool and simple thing to make if you are having friends over or if it's a hot day and you want to make a super-simple-fun ice lolly.

you'll need...

Fizzy Lemonade
Haribo sweets
Ice lolly tray

now make it....

Fill the ice lolly holder about halfway up with lemonade. You could use coke or tango or other fizzy juices but lemonade is good because it's clear and means you can see the Haribo sweets inside.

Then start adding some sweets to the lemonade. No need to pack them in too tightly, about 5-10 is probably enough but you can add more if you want to. Once you've got as many as you want in there make sure the lemonade is near the top of the mould (add some more if you need to) and then put the lid/stick on.

Place in the freezer and leave overnight or until completely frozen through. What could be easier? Now get licking!!

super simple watermelon Ice Pops

These watermelon ice pops are so quick and easy to make and perfect for summertime sleepovers.

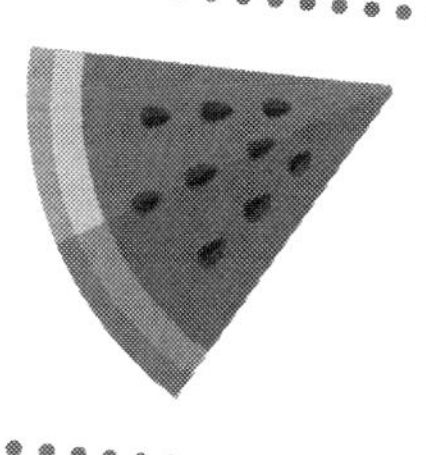

you'll need...

A couple of watermelon slices
Ice-lolly sticks
space in your freezer

cut the watermelon into triangular pieces about the size of a small pizza slice.

use a knife to make a slit in the skin part at the bottom of each triangle and push in an ice-lolly stick.

stand your watermelon lollies up stick-first in a cup or jug and place them in the freezer and leave for a couple of hours until they are frozen through.

This is easily the cheapest healthiest ice-lolly in town.

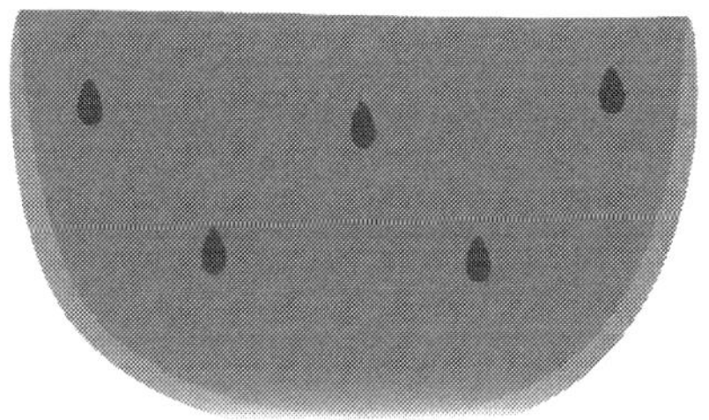

This make it happen map is a fab way of being able to visualize your travel dreams right there on your bedroom wall. It's super-easy to make and cheap too, as you can pick up really inexpensive posters of maps on the high street for not much money at all.

Make It Happen Map

Map of the world
one set of yellow pins
one set of red pins
Postcard size piece of card
Marker pen

Stick your map up on the wall.
Take your marker pen and write on your postcard

PLACES I'VE BEEN

PLACES I WANT TO GO

Then stick the card onto your map (somewhere blue in the middle of an ocean is good).

Once it's up put a red pin bedside PLACES I'VE BEEN and a yellow pin beside PLACES I WANT TO GO.

Then stick red pins into all the countries and cities on the map that you have already visited (don't worry if that's not many you've got your whole life ahead of you).

Now comes the fun part start planning your future adventures. Place a yellow pin into all the cities and countries you are want to visit. It's a really cool way of letting your imagination take you places. Every time you hear someone mention a city or a place that sounds interesting just grab a pin and stick it in. You'll get ideas from films, friends, books, just keep you ears open.

Pretty soon you'll have a map which will be full of pins - each one an adventure there for you to discover in your life. Now just live it!!

Tin can candle

Warning: Please be super-careful with this candle. Always get permission from your parents, or responsible adult, before using matches and never leave a naked flame unattended. Don't touch the tin can after the candle has been lit in case it gets hot

you'll need...

Empty tin can (use a shallow tin about 7OZ)
A regular candle

now make it....

First make sure you have thoroughly washed out your tin. Then you'll need to start melting down your candle: do this by putting the candle inside a metal bowl which is sitting in a pan of water. Put the pan on a high heat and watch over it as it melts.

Once the candle melts pull out the wick and put it in the centre of the tin can using a small amount of wax to stick it down. Then you can pour in your wax, wait for it to set and you're good to go.

Tip: you'll need to trim the wick to your desired length once set!

Marshmallow Mini Bites

These mini melted chocolate bites are divine! Make them to hand out to your friends as an epic sleepover snack or as a party treat.

you'll need...

1 bag of marshmallows
1 x 7oz bar of milk chocolate broken up into pieces (use good quality chocolate)
Mini cake cases

Gently melt the chocolate. The best way to do this is to place it in a glass bowl which is sitting over a pan of simmering water ..it's quite boring though waiting for all the chocolate to slowly melt so you could just cheat by putting it in a bowl and whacking it in the microwave. Heat it for just a few seconds at a time though, checking each time to make sure it's melting but not burning.

Use a teaspoon to add a blob of melted chocolate to each cake case. Place the marshmallow on top and add another blob of chocolate to the top. Leave to cool and get ready to eat as soon as the chocolate sets.

Sooooooo easy and proof that sometimes the simplest things are superb.

1 ....

2 ....

3 ....

4 ....

5 ....

6 ....

7 ....

8 ....

9 ....

10 ....

FILM

FILM

FILM

Must see Movies

everyone has their....

.....own list of favourite movies and there really is no right answer to the question what is the best film ever? But here's a list of a few movies you have just got to see. so what are you waiting for? Grab some pillows & popcorn and settle down to some of these killer films.

Pitch Perfect 1 & 2

These films have got the best one-liners ever!

Freaky Friday

This is hilarious. The story has been told lots of times before but the version with Jamie Lee Curtis and Lindsay Lohan is the best.

Mean Girls

This is the ultimate teen high school film. Epic.

Bring It On

Go for the latest version with Hayden Pantiettiere. Funny, touching and brilliant gymnastics.

Make your own 'must see' movie list on the page opposite.

Love is in my heart

Homemade Nutella Hot Chocolate

you'll need...

1 mug of milk
2 or 3 tablespoons of Nutella
whipped cream
saucepan
whisk

now make it....

Add about half the milk to a pan and gently warm on a medium heat. Add as much of the nutella as you want to use (use all 3 tablespoons if you want it really chocolatey) and whisk it to combine everything together really well.

When it's nice and smooth add the rest of the milk and keep on stirring until the nutella is all melted. Make sure the milk doesn't burn and when it's hot enough pour it into your mug and top with whipped cream. Perfect on a cold day if you just want to snuggle up and chill with your favourite youtube channels.

1 Hour Strengthening Hair Repair

This is a great anti frizz hair mask which is really easy to make and apply.

1 ripe banana
3 teaspoons extra virgin olive oil
½ cup milk
1 Egg

Peel the banana, break into pieces in a bowl and use a fork to mash it into a really creamy paste. Add the olive oil, milk and egg and mix it up until everything is combined.

When it's ready stand in front of a mirror and start working it into the ends of your hair. Work your way up and carry on applying to the top of your head and all the way down the back and sides of your hair. Work it right through and keep looking in the mirror to make sure you are getting all your hair covered

When you have really worked it in well braid your hair and leave it for an hour.

After the hour is up jump in the shower and give your hair a good wash with your usual shampoo and conditioner and you should have strong frizz-free hair!

oreo sprinkle pops

Tip: Try making this with mini oreos and mini lollipop sticks SOOOOOO CUTE!!!.

carefully pull your oreos apart so you have two halves, the cream filling inside should stick to one side.

Put a blob of icing on top of the cream filling and press the lollipop stick to the icing. cover with the lid of the other oreo half and make sure they are stuck firm together to make a lollipop.

Once the stick is firm cover one side of the oreo lollipop with some more of the icing and add sprinkles. super-cool and super-easy.

oreo cookies
Ice-lolly sticks
Ready made icing (or make your own)
sprinkles

ZZZZZZ

Chocolate Strawberry Overnight Oat Jar

you'll need...

4oz porridge oats
½ cup milk
2 tablespoons Greek yoghurt
1 tablespoon runny honey
2 teaspoons cocoa powder
1 small handful of chopped strawberries
1 teaspoon chocolate curls
Mason jar

Make this easy-peasy protein packed breakfast by layering your ingredients in the jar, not just because it looks pretty (which it does) but because it's the best way to store your mix overnight.

Go with oats first in the base of the jar followed by milk, yogurt, honey, cocoa powder and fresh strawberries. Finish with a sprinkle of chocolate curls and place in the fridge overnight. Now wait!

When the morning finally comes jump out of bed and dig into your delicious healthy morning oats - eat straight from the jar if you want to look cool or tip it out into a bowl.

Tasty AND good for you!

Pineapple Ice Crush Juice

This is a cool refreshing drink which is just as good to enjoy at breakfast time as it is lounging in the sun beside the pool.

you'll need...

1 apple
7oz pineapple chunks
Handful of ice cubes
¼ cup water (use more or less to get the consistency the way you like it)
Blender

Rinse all the ingredients well. Peel, core and chop the apple. Add the chopped apple and pineapple to the blender. Top up with the ice and a dash of water.
Twist on the blade and blend until smooth.

Tip: Fresh pineapple is good but tinned will work just as well.

I
pizza

Pepperoni Pitta Pizza Snack

you'll need...

1 pitta bread
1-2 teaspoons tomato purée
2 tablespoons grated cheese
A handful pepperoni slices (or whatever salami you like)

Here's a way to make a homemade pizza type snack without any of the hassle of making dough.

While you are getting everything ready switch on the oven to 200C/180C fan/gas 6

now make it....

Spread one side of the pitta with the tomato purée. Top with the cheese and place the pepperoni slices on top.

Sit the pitta on a baking sheet and bake for 10 minutes or until the cheese has melted and the peperoni is sizzling hot. Grab the ketchup and eat up.

It's no Dominos but it's cool, quick and easy.

Rainbow Ice Cubes

you'll need...

Ice cube tray
Natural Food colouring
Natural food flavouring (not essential)

now make it....

First decide how many different coloured ice cubes you are going to make. It would be AMAZING to do all the colours of the rainbow but unless you already have lots of food colouring and flavouring in the cupboard that's probably going to be too expensive, so maybe just pick one or two really bright colours you want to make and stick with those.

Making the ice cubes couldn't be simpler ..put a cup of water in a jug, add a couple of drops of colouring and a couple of drops of flavouring. Give the water a little stir and carefully pour into the ice cube tray.

Place in the freezer and leave for a few hours until completely frozen through. Fill up a glass (or a mason jar if you've got one) with some water, drop your coloured ice cubs in and enjoy.

Tip: use whichever combination of colours and flavours you like, or keep it simple and just use the same flavouring for all the colours.

DIY Pore Strip

This is a super-cool, natural way of cleansing your skin and getting rid of all those nasty little blackheads which clog up the pores.

you'll need...

Hot water (from the tap not kettle)
Towel
Toilet Paper
1 Egg
Brush

First gently pat down your face with a towel or flannel which you have dipped into hot water. This will help to open the pores in your skin.

Then break the egg and separate the yolk as it's only the egg white which you'll be using.

Take a section of toilet paper (just one piece is enough) and split the two layers so that you are left with 2 very thin pieces.

Take your brush and apply the egg white over your face wherever you have any blackheads (this mostly will be around your nose area but it can be on your chin, forehead etc). Then take the thin toilet paper pieces and spread them over your face so they stick to the egg white. Brush more egg white over the top and leave to harden for at least 10 minutes.

After this time gently peel off the paper and take a look at what you have just pulled out of your skin. Try to do this a couple of times a week and your skin will be clear & glowing.

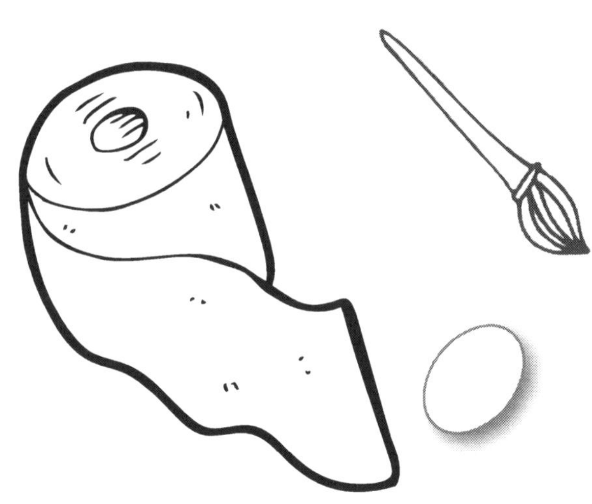

Rainbow Fruit Kebabs

This is such a simple thing to make and it is an absolutely delicious healthy snack which makes a great alternative to some of the sweet stuff we all love to have too much of.

If you are only making one kebab you'll only need one of each of the ingredients listed.

you'll need...

fresh raspberries
fresh strawberries
fresh tangerine segments
fresh cubed mango
fresh green grapes
fresh red grapes
fresh blueberries
wooden skewers

Take your wooden skewer and thread a piece of each fruit in turn to make the tastiest healthiest kebab around. Mix up the colours to make sure you get a lovely rainbow effect and if you make a few kebabs rather than just one they look really impressive to serve at a party or sleepover.

Girls Night In........

essentials:

sleepovers are always fun but here are a few of the cutest DIY's you can do to make sure yours is super special.

epic cute snacks

these are a MUST! Try making the Mini Marshallow bites on page 35!!! Get you friends over early and have fun making them or prepare everything yourself earlier so that you can impress everyone with your skills!

homemade face mask

HOMemade Face MASK - NOW it's time for some night-time routine. Mix up a DIY facemask try the honey and chocolate mask on page 19.

..........sleepover Plan

water balloon fight

start the fun outside with a fun water ballon fight. you might need to persuade your parents but if you tell them it's just five minutes of fun, you should be able to get away with it. Plus once everyone is soaking wet it's a great time to get undressed and into your jammies.

set the mood

If you want to make your room look extra special set up some cute fairy lights and switch these on when it's movie time. or even better make the fairy light lamp on page 27. Perfect! Perfect!

get Cosy

once you are done it's time to settle down with as many blankets and pillows as you can get your hands on. There is not such thing as too many! choose your movie, grab your snacks and CHILL OUT!

Plus don't forget to grab your phone so that you can show everyone how much fun you've been having.

Personalize your pencils:

This is a super fun, simple and unique way to spice up your boring pencils and the best thing is NOBODY will have the same pencils as you!

you'll need...

Regular pencils
washi tape

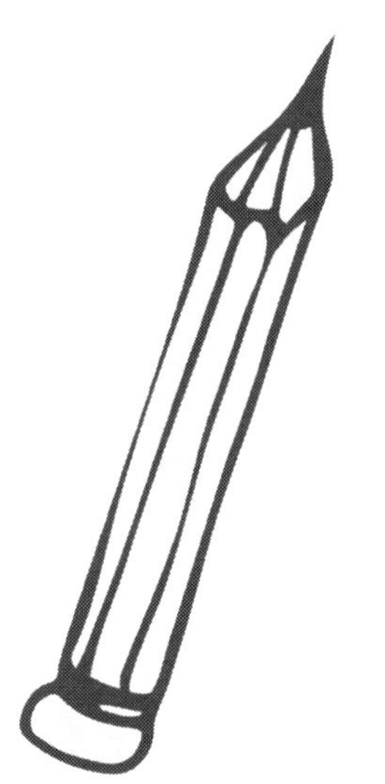

now make it....

Get your chosen colours of washi tape and grab a pencil. Then start by taking one colour and wrapping it around the top of the pencil then the next colour and wrap it underneath that. Personalize them to match your style, here are some ideas:

rainbow
black and white
zig zag pattern
single block colour!

Once you have reached the bottom (or wherever you want to stop) you have these amazing, cool and different pencils that took you about 5 minutes to make!

Starbucks Gift Cup

Everyone loves starbucks and this is a cool way to give a gift to a real starbucks lover.

you'll need...

A Frappuccino takeaway cup from starbucks (just pop in and ask for one, the staff are usually really nice and will give you a clean one for free)
Glitter
PVA glue
Paint Brush
White tissue paper
Chocolates

now make it....

Take your cup and using the starbucks logo at the front as a guide paint on a thick band of glue from front to back so that you have got a ring of glue around the cup which starts and finishes each side of the logo (but don't put any glue on the actual logo).

Pour your glitter onto this band of glue until it's completely covered and your cup now has a ring of glitter around it.

Next fill it with tissue paper and whichever chocolates you are using - something wrapped in silver or gold paper would be fab.

Pop on your lid and you've got a cool gift to give away. Remember you can use anything you like inside the cup it doesn't have to be chocolates. Let your imagination run wild!!

Fall Tea-Light Lantern

you'll need...

1 empty jam jar
A handful of fallen autumn leaves
Glue dots
Mod Podge glue
Paint brush
Tea-light

This is a really easy idea to make your room feel all autumn-y and cosy. Use fresh leaves so that they are bendy and easy to work with, old leaves will be crispy and break up easily

now make it....

Arrange your leaves on the outside of the jam jar using the glue dots. You don't need to completely cover the jar with leaves, it's nice to be able to see the outline of individual leaves rather than just a mass (small leaves are best for this).

Once you have got your leaves in the right position completely cover them, and every inch of the outside of the jar, with glue using the brush. This will really secure the leaves to the jar and give you a lovely blurry/glassy effect once the glue dries off.

Drop your tea light into the bottom of the jam jar then when night falls and it's time to get cosy, light up your tea-light and enjoy the autumn glow.

Warning: Please be super-careful with this lantern. Always get permission from your parents, or responsible adult, before using matches and never leave a naked flame unattended.

scrabble coasters!

These scrabble coasters are soooooo cute and make a great personalized gift!

you'll need...

Thick card
scrabble letter tiles
strong glue
Mod Podge glue
Brush

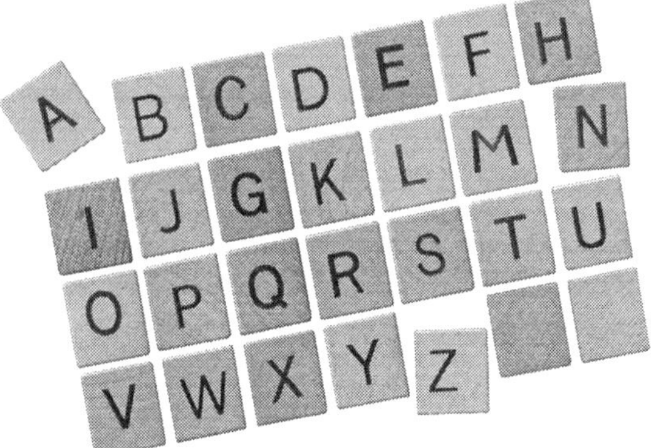

now make it....

First figure out what words you want to say on the coaster and make sure the words all have the same amount of letters in them, for example:

Arrange your letters and then cut a piece of card to exactly fit your words. once you have done that start gluing your letters to the piece of card and leave them to dry. Using a brush add a layer of Mod Podge once the letters are dry to give it a glossy waterproof seal. There you have it! A great gift or even just a cool thing to keep for yourself!

tumblr Phone cases

This is a simple tip on how to get interchangeable images on your phone case so that you can switch up your look anytime you like.

now make it....

The first thing to do is to go onto google, find a picture of your phone and cut it out. You should easily be able to be a template which will be the exact size of your phone and have the camera in the right place etc. once you have printed it, cut it out and lay it on top of your coloured paper. cut out the coloured paper to match the template so that you now have a coloured base which will sit in the back of your clear case.

Now all you need to do is go onto google images and search tumblr png
choose a picture you like, and set up the image to print. You might need to alter the scale if it's going to print out too big, just guess it until you get it right. It doesn't have to be an exact fit as you've got your background template cover to sit it on.

cut out your image and insert it into your phone case with the coloured template as your background. Add a glue dot if you want your image to stick in an exact place but it will probably be fine without it as the phone will hold it there.

The great thing about this is you can do the exact same thing with your ipad or tablet too as long as you have a clear protective case to work with.

you'll need...

Google
Printer
1 sheet coloured paper
1 sheet white paper
clear case for your phone

Family
Tree
Take everything you learned and add some pictures/illustrations to your family tree craft project to show what you have learned.
Learning where you come from means you know more about yourself and it's actually pretty cool hearing about the olden days before youtube existed!

Family Tree

you might have seen......

shows on TV where people try to find out more about their family and work out who their long lost relatives are.

Online you'll find loads of free tools, templates and craft projects to help you make a family tree like the mini one on the opposite page. It's a fun thing to do and you can frame your finished tree as a cool craft idea to keep in your room.

Finding more out about your family takes detective work and a good way to try to discover more is to talk to older relatives in your family. They can tell you their memories of your family from before you were born.

If you want to get serious and find out more than just the names of your ancestors try delving in a bit deeper and interviewing an older relative. In person is best, but you can do it over the phone too.

Here are some questions you could ask to find out more about them and in turn you'll find out something new about yourself too.

1. Where did you grow up and what was it like?
2. What were your parents' and siblings' names? Were you an oldest, youngest or middle child?
3. Where did your parents work?
4. What did you do for fun?
5. What are your happiest family memories?
6. How did you meet the person you married?
7. What do you remember about your grandparents?
8. Do you know any stories about our ancestors? Where did they come from?
9. Do you have any old photos or papers you could show me?

De-stress......

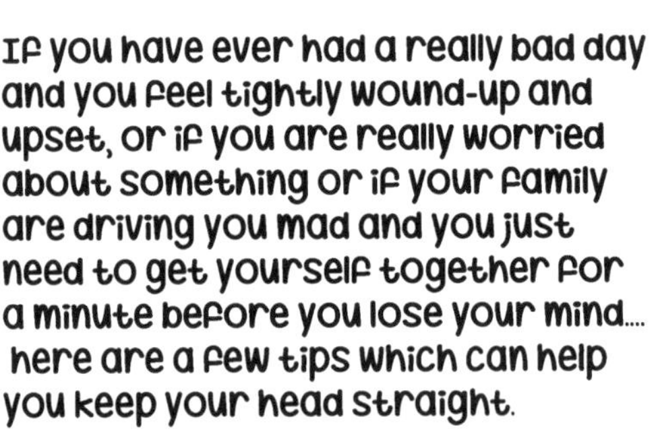

If you have ever had a really bad day and you feel tightly wound-up and upset, or if you are really worried about something or if your family are driving you mad and you just need to get yourself together for a minute before you lose your mind.... here are a few tips which can help you keep your head straight.

First find a quiet place to sit, it's best if you can just get away from everyone. That's all you need to do to get started but you could also close the curtains if you like and light a scented candle to really set the mood.

Once you are sitting, try to settle down and continue to breathe normally.

Now try a deep breath: breathe in slowly through your nose, allowing your chest to rise as you fill your lungs. Hold your breath for a couple of seconds before breathing out slowly through your mouth.

......Relaxation Tips

Wait 2-3 seconds before taking another breath and then repeat for at least 5 to 10 breaths until you feel things calming down.

While you are doing this try really hard not to think about anything but your breathing. Let your mind be clear and really concentrate on the calming effect the breathing will have on you.

Pretty soon you should be feeling more relaxed and able to deal with what's going on. Do it for as long or as little as you like.

Tip: Try closing your eyes when you are doing your breathing, it can really help to shut everything out.

31563487R00038

Made in the USA
Middletown, DE
04 May 2016